PIRATE TR

It is 1607. Tom Creek's pirate boat, The Black Star, goes down in the sea. Tom Creek loses all his treasure. As the boat goes down he shouts, 'This is my treasure and no other man's. I curse this treasure – forever.'

Many years pass. Many men try to get the treasure. Many men die.

It is 2009. There is a new expedition to the Black Star. The boat is called The Sardine. John West, his wife Mae, and their friends want to get the treasure. They are not afraid of Tom Creek's curse. Some of them think there is no curse.

Are they right or are they mad?

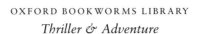

OXFORD BOOKWORMS LIBRARY
Thriller & Adventure

Pirate Treasure

Starter (250 headwords)

PHILLIP BURROWS AND MARK FOSTER

Pirate Treasure

OXFORD UNIVERSITY PRESS

OXFORD
UNIVERSITY PRESS

Great Clarendon Street, Oxford OX2 6DP

Oxford University Press is a department of the University of Oxford.
It furthers the University's objective of excellence in research, scholarship,
and education by publishing worldwide in

Oxford New York

Auckland Cape Town Dar es Salaam Hong Kong Karachi
Kuala Lumpur Madrid Melbourne Mexico City Nairobi
New Delhi Shanghai Taipei Toronto

With offices in

Argentina Austria Brazil Chile Czech Republic France Greece
Guatemala Hungary Italy Japan Poland Portugal Singapore
South Korea Switzerland Thailand Turkey Ukraine Vietnam

oxford and oxford english are registered trade marks of
Oxford University Press in the UK and in certain other countries

ISBN: 978 0 19 479364 3

Printed in China

This book is printed on paper from certified and well-managed sources.

Word count (main text): 950

For more information on the Oxford Bookworms Library,
visit www.oup.com/bookworms

CONTENTS

PIRATE TREASURE

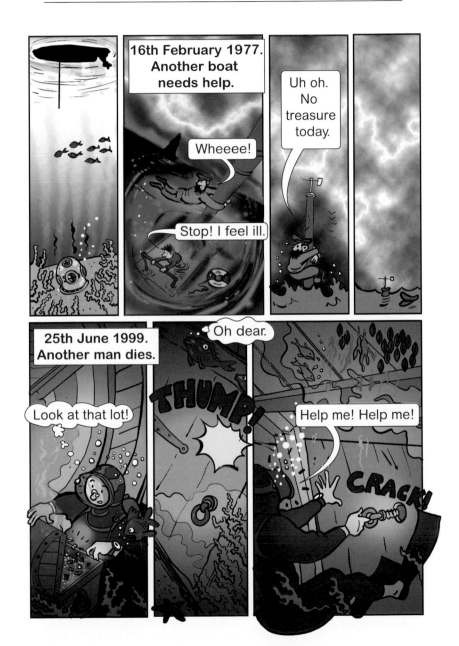

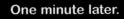

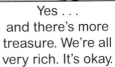

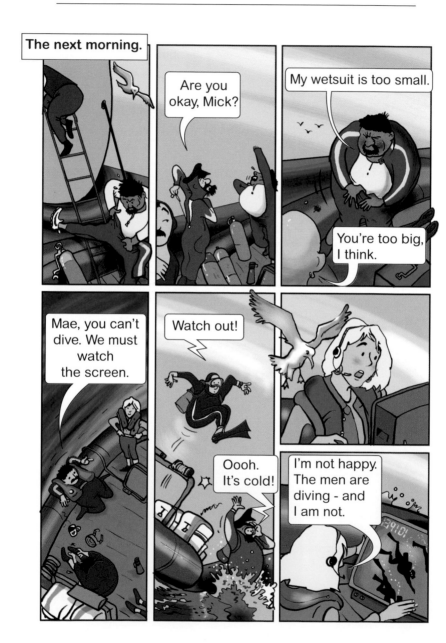

John, there's trouble.

Aghh . . . my foot!

It's okay. You're safe now.

Help him up.

Be careful. I think his foot is broken.

Thanks, boys.

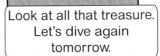

Look at all that treasure. Let's dive again tomorrow.

The next day.

More breakfast.

Okay. Mick can't dive today, but I can.

Be careful, John. The Black Star is bad.

Later that morning.

This is easy. There's lots of treasure.

Can cats swim?

OW!

Do you need help?

I'm okay. It's nothing.

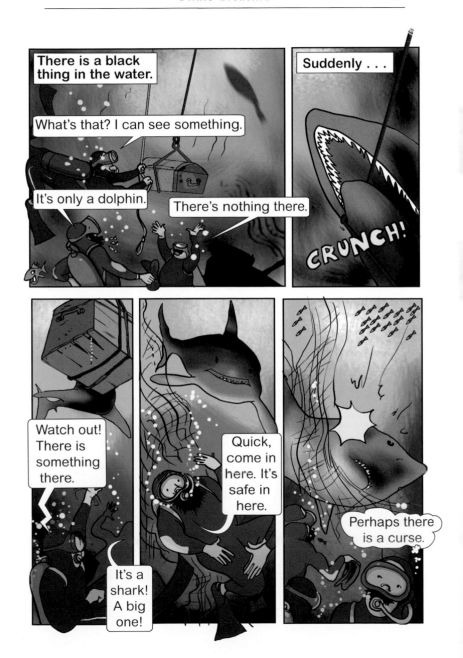

Back in the boat.

What do we do now?

I don't know.

I know.

You men! I understand Tom Creek's curse now. I know what to do.

Mae! Come back! There's a shark in the water.

Mae!

Come back!

GLUG GLUG GLUG

There's more than one shark, John. Look at this.

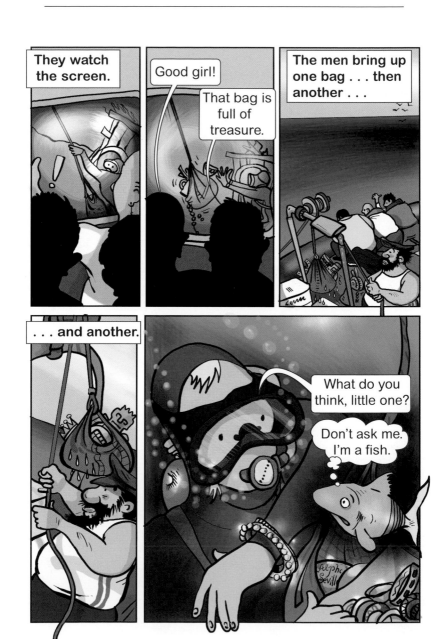

Pirate Treasure

ACTIVITIES

ACTIVITIES

Before Reading

1 Look at the front and back cover of the book. Now answer these questions.

1 What is John West looking for?
a ☐ Treasure.
b ☐ Fish.
c ☐ Love.

2 Where is he looking?
a ☐ Up a hill.
b ☐ Under the sea.
c ☐ In a city.

3 Who is Tom Creek?
a ☐ A diver.
b ☐ John West's friend.
c ☐ A pirate.

2 Guess what happens. In the story . . .   *Yes*   *No*

1 Tom Creek loses some treasure.   ☐   ☐
2 Tom Creek finds some treasure.   ☐   ☐
3 John West's friends run away.   ☐   ☐
4 they see a dolphin.   ☐   ☐

ACTIVITIES

While Reading

1 Read pages 1–3, and answer these questions.

1 When does The Black Star go down?
2 Who says 'I curse this treasure forever'?
3 When does a big wave hit a boat?
4 When does a door shut under the sea?

2 Read pages 4–6. What are the missing words?

1 'Tomorrow they are going to find The Black Star's _____.'
a ☐ treasure   b ☐ pirate   c ☐ sandwiches

2 'Are you mad? There is no _____.'
a ☐ shark   b ☐ sun   c ☐ curse

3 'We are all good _____. Let's find the treasure.'
a ☐ pirates   b ☐ men   c ☐ divers

4 'Don't go to The Black Star. My men . . . they are all _____.'
a ☐ angry   b ☐ dead   c ☐ afraid

3 Read pages 7–11, and answer these questions.

1 How does Barry Barnes leave the room?
2 Who sees a dolphin?
3 What can they see on the screen?
4 Why can't they dive today?

4 Read pages 12–15, and answer these questions.

1 On page 12, why does John say, 'Mae, you can't dive'?

2 On page 13, why does John say, 'That doesn't look good'?

3 On page 14, why does the diver say, 'Look at that'?

4 On page 15, why does Mae say, 'John, there's trouble'?

5 Read pages 16–19. Are these sentences true or false?

	T	F
1 John thinks The Black Star is bad.	☐	☐
2 They can see a dolphin in the water.	☐	☐
3 They run away from the shark.	☐	☐
4 The shark sees some blood.	☐	☐

6 Read pages 20–24, and answer these questions.

1 On page 20, why does John say, 'Mae, come back'?

2 On page 21, why does Mae say, 'They aren't interested in me'?

3 On page 22, why does Mae ask, 'What do you think, little one'?

4 On page 23, why does Mae say, 'No more. I'm too tired'?

5 On page 24, why does the dolphin say, 'Ow! It's them again'?

ACTIVITIES

After Reading

1 Tell the story to a friend. Use these words.

pirate / boat / curse / dead / treasure / shark / dolphin / woman / dive / expedition

2 Fill in the speech bubbles to write a different ending.

3 Put these speech bubbles in the correct order. Number them 1–6.

a ☐ ' . . . But I am a *woman*.'

b ☐ 'Don't be afraid of the shark. I know what to do.'

c ☐ 'Fight them boys. The Black Star is our boat.'

d ☐ 'I can't stay here. I must find her now.'

e ☐ 'Be careful. I think his foot is broken.'

f ☐ 'Hey! You really are dead.'

4 Match the beginnings and endings of these sentences.

1 The Black Star is . . .

2 John West tries to get the treasure . . .

3 John cuts his hand . . .

4 Mae is not hurt by the curse . . .

5 The dolphin does . . .

a) and a shark comes.

b) not get a fish.

c) Tom Creek's pirate boat.

d) in his boat, The Sardine.

e) because she is a woman.

ABOUT THE AUTHORS

Mark Foster and Phillip Burrows have worked as a writer / illustrator team since 1991. They were born three years and many miles apart, but they are very nearly twins. They drive the same car, work on the same computers, and wear the same wellington boots - but not at the same time! They spend all the money they get from writing on gadgets, but please don't tell their wives. Mark and Phill have worked together on several Bookworms titles, including *Taxi of Terror*, *Orca*, and *Last Chance* (Starters). When they meet to write, they like to go to expensive hotels, eat chips dipped in coffee, and laugh at their own jokes.

OXFORD BOOKWORMS LIBRARY

Classics • Crime & Mystery • Factfiles • Fantasy & Horror
Human Interest • Playscripts • Thriller & Adventure
True Stories • World Stories

The OXFORD BOOKWORMS LIBRARY provides enjoyable reading in English, with a wide range of classic and modern fiction, non-fiction, and plays. It includes original and adapted texts in seven carefully graded language stages, which take learners from beginner to advanced level. An overview is given on the next pages.

All Stage 1 titles are available as audio recordings, as well as over eighty other titles from Starter to Stage 6. All Starters and many titles at Stages 1 to 4 are specially recommended for younger learners. Every Bookworm is illustrated, and Starters and Factfiles have full-colour illustrations.

The OXFORD BOOKWORMS LIBRARY also offers extensive support. Each book contains an introduction to the story, notes about the author, a glossary, and activities. Additional resources include tests and worksheets, and answers for these and for the activities in the books. There is advice on running a class library, using audio recordings, and the many ways of using Oxford Bookworms in reading programmes. Resource materials are available on the website <www.oup.com/bookworms>.

The *Oxford Bookworms Collection* is a series for advanced learners. It consists of volumes of short stories by well-known authors, both classic and modern. Texts are not abridged or adapted in any way, but carefully selected to be accessible to the advanced student.

You can find details and a full list of titles in the *Oxford Bookworms Library Catalogue* and *Oxford English Language Teaching Catalogues*, and on the website <www.oup.com/bookworms>.

THE OXFORD BOOKWORMS LIBRARY
GRADING AND SAMPLE EXTRACTS

STARTER • 250 HEADWORDS

present simple – present continuous – imperative –
can/cannot, must – *going to* (future) – simple gerunds …

Her phone is ringing – but where is it?
Sally gets out of bed and looks in her bag. No phone.
She looks under the bed. No phone. Then she looks
behind the door. There is her phone. Sally picks up her
phone and answers it. *Sally's Phone*

STAGE 1 • 400 HEADWORDS

… past simple – coordination with *and*, *but*, *or* –
subordination with *before*, *after*, *when*, *because*, *so* …

I knew him in Persia. He was a famous builder and I
worked with him there. For a time I was his friend, but
not for long. When he came to Paris, I came after him –
I wanted to watch him. He was a very clever, very
dangerous man. *The Phantom of the Opera*

STAGE 2 • 700 HEADWORDS

… present perfect – *will* (future) – *(don't) have to*, *must not*, *could* –
comparison of adjectives – simple *if* clauses – past continuous –
tag questions – *ask/tell* + infinitive …

While I was writing these words in my diary, I decided
what to do. I must try to escape. I shall try to get down
the wall outside. The window is high above the ground,
but I have to try. I shall take some of the gold with me – if
I escape, perhaps it will be helpful later. *Dracula*

STAGE 3 • 1000 HEADWORDS

... should, may – present perfect continuous – *used to* – past perfect – causative – relative clauses – indirect statements ...

Of course, it was most important that no one should see Colin, Mary, or Dickon entering the secret garden. So Colin gave orders to the gardeners that they must all keep away from that part of the garden in future. *The Secret Garden*

STAGE 4 • 1400 HEADWORDS

... past perfect continuous – passive (simple forms) – *would* conditional clauses – indirect questions – relatives with *where/when* – gerunds after prepositions/phrases ...

I was glad. Now Hyde could not show his face to the world again. If he did, every honest man in London would be proud to report him to the police. *Dr Jekyll and Mr Hyde*

STAGE 5 • 1800 HEADWORDS

... future continuous – future perfect – passive (modals, continuous forms) – *would have* conditional clauses – modals + perfect infinitive ...

If he had spoken Estella's name, I would have hit him. I was so angry with him, and so depressed about my future, that I could not eat the breakfast. Instead I went straight to the old house. *Great Expectations*

STAGE 6 • 2500 HEADWORDS

... passive (infinitives, gerunds) – advanced modal meanings – clauses of concession, condition

When I stepped up to the piano, I was confident. It was as if I knew that the prodigy side of me really did exist. And when I started to play, I was so caught up in how lovely I looked that I didn't worry how I would sound. *The Joy Luck Club*

BOOKWORMS · THRILLER & ADVENTURE · STARTER

Escape

PHILLIP BURROWS AND MARK FOSTER

'I'm not a thief. I'm an innocent man,' shouts Brown. He is angry because he is in prison and the prison guards hate him. Then one day Brown has an idea. It is dangerous – very dangerous.

BOOKWORMS · THRILLER & ADVENTURE · STARTER

Orca

PHILLIP BURROWS AND MARK FOSTER

When Tonya and her friends decide to sail around the world they want to see exciting things and visit exciting places.

But one day, they meet an orca – a killer whale – one of the most dangerous animals in the sea. And life gets a little too exciting.

BOOKWORMS · THRILLER & ADVENTURE · STARTER
Taxi of Terror
PHILLIP BURROWS AND MARK FOSTER

'How does it work?' Jack asks when he opens his present – a mobile phone. Later that night, Jack is a prisoner in a taxi in the empty streets of the dark city. He now tries his mobile phone for the first time. Can it save his life?

BOOKWORMS · THRILLER & ADVENTURE · STARTER
Last Chance
PHILLIP BURROWS AND MARK FOSTER

'How can Mr Frank be angry now?' thinks Mike happily. His film is good and he is the only cameraman on the volcano. Now he can go home. But then he finds Jenny and she is dying. Rocks start to move and Mike is afraid. Can they get off the volcano alive? And what happens to Mike's camera and film?

BOOKWORMS · HUMAN INTEREST · STARTER ·

The Girl with Red Hair

CHRISTINE LINDOP

Every day people come to Mason's store – old people, young people, men and women. From his office, and in the store, Mark watches them. And when they leave the store, he forgets them. Then one day a girl with red hair comes to the store, and everything changes for Mark. Now he can't forget that beautiful face, those green eyes, and that red hair . . .

BOOKWORMS · CRIME & MYSTERY · STARTER ·

Give us the Money

MAEVE CLARKE

'Every day is the same. Nothing exciting ever happens to me,' thinks Adam one boring Monday morning. But today is not the same. When he helps a beautiful young woman because some men want to take her bag, life gets exciting and very, very dangerous.